D1708068

Claymation
Sensation

MONSTER CLAYMATION

Emily Reid

WINDMILL
BOOKS

Published in 2017 by **Windmill Books**,
an Imprint of Rosen Publishing
29 East 21st Street, New York, NY 10010

Produced for Rosen by BlueAppleWorks Inc.

Creative Director: Melissa McClellan
Managing Editor for BlueAppleWorks: Melissa McClellan
Design: T.J. Choleva
Editor: Kelly Spence
Puppet Artisans: Sarah Hodgins (p. 8, 14); Janet Kompare-Fritz (p. 18, 22, 26); Jane Yates (p. 10, 13, 16, 20)

Picture credits: plasticine letters:Vitaly Korovin/Shutterstock; title page, TOC, Austen Photography; p. 4 Sony Pictures
Releasing/Photofest; p.5 Janet Kompare-Fritz; ; p. 6 left to right and top to bottom: ukrfidget/Shutterstock; Andrey Eremin/
Shutterstock; exopixel /Shutterstock; Lukas Gojda/Shutterstock; jocic/Shutterstock; koosen/Shutterstock; Irina Nartova/
Shutterstock; STILLFX/Shutterstock; Darryl Brooks/Shutterstock; Winai Tepsuttinun/Shutterstock; Yulia elf_inc Tropina/
Shutterstock; Austen Photography; All For You /Shutterstock; Radu Bercan /Shutterstock; Austen Photography; p. 7 left to
right and top to bottom: Ilike/Shutterstock; Tarzhanova/Shutterstock; Austen Photography; kamomeen /Shutterstock; Lesha/
Shutterstock; ikurdyumov/Shutterstock; Austen Photography; Ilike/Shutterstock; p-8 to 27 Austen Photography; p. 28 left
Valentina Razumova/Shutterstock; p. 29 upper left Warongdech/Shutterstock;p. 29 top right Anneka/Shutterstock; p. 29 right
taelove7/Shutterstock; p. 30, 31 Austen Photography

Cataloging-in-Publication Data
Names: Reid, Emily.
Title: Monster claymation / Emily Reid.
Description: New York : Windmill Books, 2017. | Series: Claymation sensation | Includes index.
Identifiers: ISBN 9781508192039 (pbk.) | ISBN 9781508192008 (library bound) | ISBN 9781508191940 (6 pack)
Subjects: LCSH: Animation (Cinematography)--Juvenile literature. | Sculpture--Technique--Juvenile literature.|
    Monsters in art--Juvenile literature.
Classification: LCC TR897.5 R45 2017 | DDC 777'.7--dc23

Manufactured in the United States of America
CPSIA Compliance Information: Batch #BS16PK: For Further Information contact Rosen Publishing, New York, New York at 1-800-237-9932

Contents

What Is Claymation?   4

Materials and Techniques   6

Body Parts and Armatures   8

Facial Expressions and Body Language   10

Monster Blob   12

Troll Puppet   14

Stick Puppet   16

Mummy Puppet   18

Zombie Puppet   20

Ogre Puppet   22

The Props   24

The Set   26

Lights, Camera, . . .   28

. . . Action! Making Your Movie   30

Glossary   32

For More Information   32

Index   32

What Is Claymation?

Get ready to scare up some fun making your very own monster Claymation! Claymation, also known as clay **animation**, combines **stop-motion** animation with characters or puppets made out of modeling clay to create movies or short videos.

Stop-motion animation creates the illusion of movement when a series of still images, called **frames**, are quickly played in sequence. Each frame shows a slight change in position from the previous frame. Clay characters are easy to move and reposition to show these actions in small steps. The smaller the movements, the smoother the sequence appears. It takes several frames to make a Claymation movie. Animations can be created using many devices, including a traditional camera, smartphone, or tablet.

The Pirates! Band of Misfits *is a 3-D Claymation movie that was released in 2012. It used extremely detailed puppets. For each frame, animators had to carefully position each puppet. It took about a week to shoot just six seconds of footage!*

Claymation Tip

There are lots of apps you can use to create your Claymation movie. These apps let you shoot and edit your movie using one device. Make sure to ask permission before you download any apps to your smartphone, tablet, or computer.

All types of filmmaking, including Claymation, tell a story. To start, brainstorm an idea for your monster movie. Think of a beginning, middle, and end. Write a short summary of the story. How many characters do you need to tell your story? What kind of background and props will you use?

When you make a Claymation movie, it is important to map out the character's movements before you start shooting. A **storyboard** is a series of drawings that show each step of the story. Use a storyboard to figure out what actions are needed, and in what order, to tell your story from start to finish. Sketch out each scene and label it with the scene number. After the storyboard is ready, it's time to create your puppets.

A storyboard showing six frames.

Scene 1

Scene 2

Scene 3

Scene 4

Scene 5

Scene 6

Materials and Techniques

Claymation puppets are created with nondrying, oil-based clay. Plasticine is a popular brand, although any nondrying modeling clay will do. This type of clay is moldable enough to create a character, flexible enough to allow that character to move in many ways, and dense enough to hold its shape when combined with a wire **armature**.

Materials That You Will Need

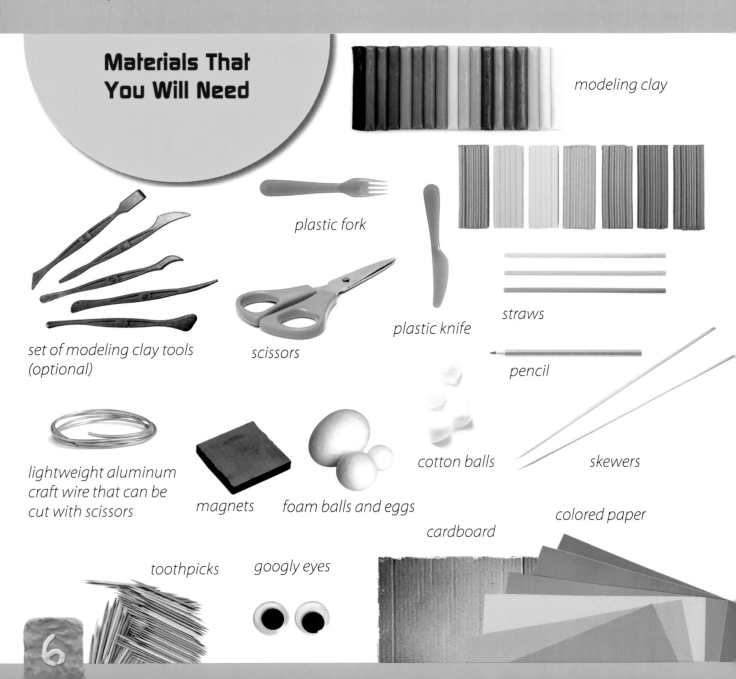

modeling clay

plastic fork

set of modeling clay tools (optional)

scissors

plastic knife

straws

pencil

lightweight aluminum craft wire that can be cut with scissors

magnets

foam balls and eggs

cotton balls

skewers

cardboard

colored paper

toothpicks

googly eyes

Working with Clay

Modeling clay is oily and can be messy to work with. Prepare a work area. A piece of cardboard or foam board is great to work on. Wash your hands well when you finish working, as they will be oily, too.

Basic Shapes

All of these shapes can be made big or small or thin or thick, depending on the amount of clay used and the pressure applied. Use your fingers to squish, smooth, pinch, flatten, and poke the clay into whatever shape you want.

To form a ball, move your hands in a circle while pressing the clay lightly between them.

To create a pancake shape, roll a ball and flatten it between your thumb and fingers. Smooth the edges if they crack.

To make a snake shape, roll the clay on a flat surface with your fingers.

To form a teardrop, pinch and roll one end of a ball into a point.

To create a cylinder, roll a large piece of clay in your hand, then roll it on a flat surface to smooth. Press each end into the table to flatten it.

To make a slab, start with a large piece and flatten it on your work surface. Keep pressing the clay out and away from the center until it is as flat as you want it.

Modeling Tips

● Always start by kneading the clay in your hands to warm it up and soften it.

● You can mix different colors together to create new colors. Just squish the clay in your hands until it is blended completely or leave it partially blended to create a marble effect.

● Make your puppets about the same size as an action figure, between 4 and 6 inches (10 and 15 cm) tall. They should be big enough to move around but not so big they fall over.

7

Body Parts and Armatures

Puppets can be made in many ways. The simple ones require only modeling clay and some patience. If you decide to create more complicated puppets, you will need additional elements to give the puppets structure and support, such as wire armatures and foam shapes. It is a good idea to keep anything that is on top of the puppet light so it does not droop during animation. Using a lightweight foam ball should do the trick.

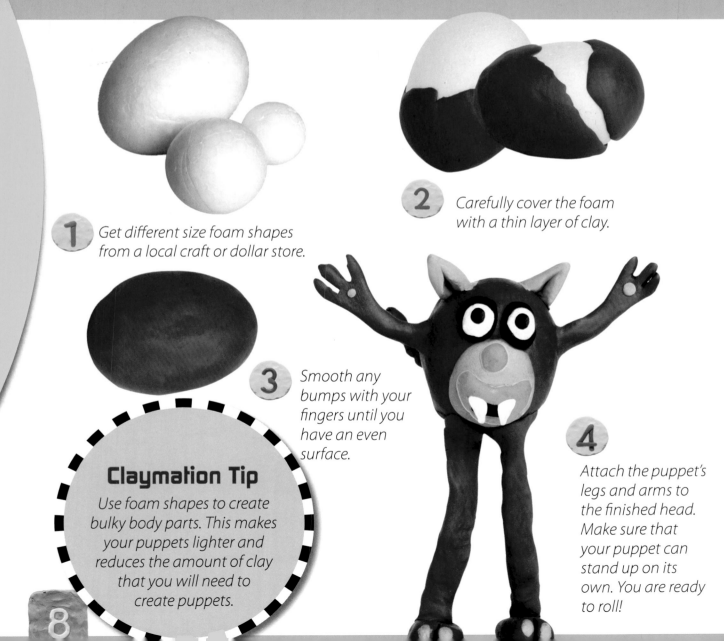

1 Get different size foam shapes from a local craft or dollar store.

2 Carefully cover the foam with a thin layer of clay.

3 Smooth any bumps with your fingers until you have an even surface.

4 Attach the puppet's legs and arms to the finished head. Make sure that your puppet can stand up on its own. You are ready to roll!

Claymation Tip

Use foam shapes to create bulky body parts. This makes your puppets lighter and reduces the amount of clay that you will need to create puppets.

Stability

Make sure your character has a big enough base or feet to support its weight. If necessary, you can stabilize it with putty or put pushpins through the puppet's feet to hold it in place.

Armatures

Armatures function as a skeleton that holds the puppet parts together and allows for them to move easily. Wire-based armatures are made using strands of lightweight wire. Whenever useful, you can combine an armature with foam pieces to create a base for your puppet. Make sure you don't make the clay too thick around the armature, or your puppet will be difficult to move.

Be creative with the details. Try new things. Use modeling tools and bits of clay to add gory touches to some of your puppets. Have fun with it!

To make an armature for a figure, start with a long piece of wire. Fold it in half. Twist the wire to form a loop at the top.

Take one piece of the wire and bend it to form one of the figure's arms. You can make it whatever length you choose. At the end of the arm, loop the wire and twist it back on itself. Repeat this step on the opposite side using the other length of wire.

Twist both wires together to form the body.

Make the legs and feet following the same steps used for the arms. If you have extra wire left, cut it off or wind it around the body.

Use a foam ball for the head to make the puppet lighter.

9

Facial Expressions and Body Language

A puppet's facial features include its eyes, nose, mouth, and eyebrows. The way these features are positioned can make your puppet look shocked or scared, happy or sad. Simply adding eyebrows can completely change the look on your puppet's face. Try some of these techniques to add expression to your Claymation characters.

Googly Eyes

Googly eyes can be pressed directly onto the puppet's face or added to a small pancake shape.

Simple Eyes

Make simple eyes by rolling two small white balls. Then flatten two smaller black balls onto the white ones for pupils.

Colored Eyes

To make colored eyes, roll two green balls, then flatten them. Roll two smaller balls in white, then two more sets of tiny balls using blue and black clay. Press the eyes together as shown.

Eyebrows

For eyebrows, use brown or black clay to roll two thin snakes. Place one over each eye. Arch the eyebrows to show surprise. Point them downward to create an angry expression.

Teeth

For teeth, cut triangles or rectangles out of a thin white slab.

Loops

Loops can be wrapped around a puppet's necks, arms, or legs. To make a loop, roll a skinny snake. Wrap it around the chosen body part. Join the ends together by gently pressing down where they overlap.

Mouth Shapes

Using certain mouth shapes is a great way to show how your character is feeling. Use thin snakes to form lips that you can easily position. You can change the puppet's expression between frames as needed.

Gloomy Expression
Make your puppet look sad by having its mouth closed and pointed downward.

Shocked Expression
Create a shocked expression by forming an O shape.

Happy Expression
Show that your puppet is happy by curving its mouth into a big smile.

Gross Expression
Show that your puppet is grossed out with a slightly open, but narrow and straight mouth shape.

Use body language to accompany your puppet's facial expressions. Try pairing some of these body positions with the above facial expressions in your Claymation movie.

Shocked Expression

To show shock, position the puppet's arms down and away from its body.

Happy Expression

To show joy, raise the puppet's arms up and away from its body.

Gloomy Expression

To show gloom, place the puppet's arms down alongside its body.

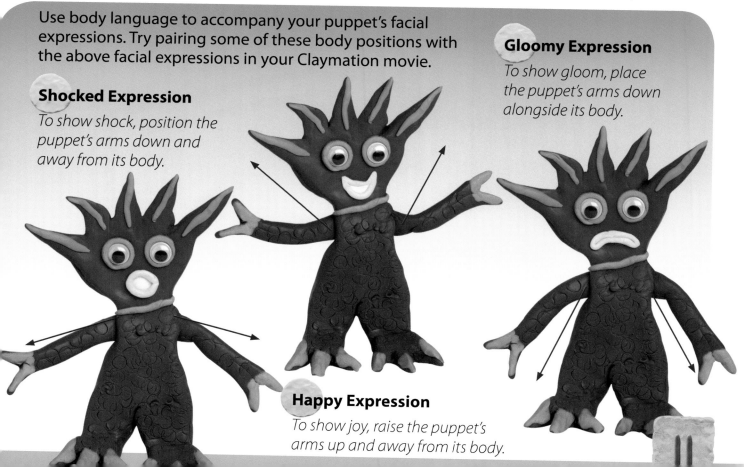

Monster Blob

Monstrous blobs appear in several scary movies. Some come from space while others emerge from deep within the Earth. Most blobs eat everything in their path. Many can even change shape. Not all blobs are evil. You can make your monster blob funny or scary, it's up to you!

1 *Use a lightweight foam ball for the monster's body. Carefully cut the ball in half using a plastic knife. Hold the halves together and push a toothpick through one end to make two holes. Remove the toothpick.*

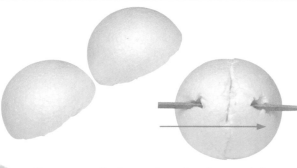

2 *Cut a small piece of craft wire and thread it through the two holes. Feed one end into the foam to join the two pieces together. Bend the remaining wire to form a tail.*

3 *Completely cover the foam and wire with a thin layer of clay. Be sure to cover the inside of the monster's mouth, too.*

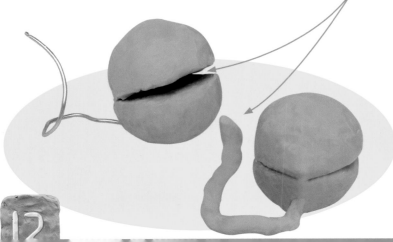

4 *Roll and flatten a long orange snake. Coil it around the monster's tail. Next, roll a short orange snake. Flatten it and press it along the center of the monster's head.*

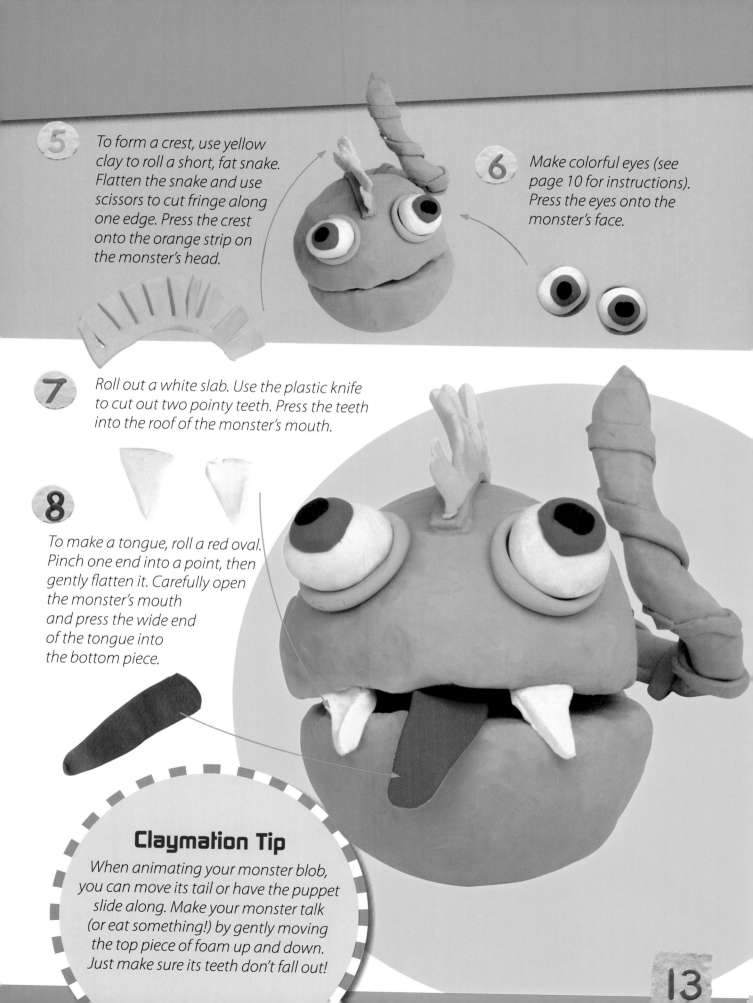

5 To form a crest, use yellow clay to roll a short, fat snake. Flatten the snake and use scissors to cut fringe along one edge. Press the crest onto the orange strip on the monster's head.

6 Make colorful eyes (see page 10 for instructions). Press the eyes onto the monster's face.

7 Roll out a white slab. Use the plastic knife to cut out two pointy teeth. Press the teeth into the roof of the monster's mouth.

8 To make a tongue, roll a red oval. Pinch one end into a point, then gently flatten it. Carefully open the monster's mouth and press the wide end of the tongue into the bottom piece.

Claymation Tip

When animating your monster blob, you can move its tail or have the puppet slide along. Make your monster talk (or eat something!) by gently moving the top piece of foam up and down. Just make sure its teeth don't fall out!

Troll Puppet

Trolls are mythical creatures from the ancient Norse culture. In many stories, they live in remote places far from humans. Some are not particularly friendly and turn into stone in the sunlight. Others, like this troll, are nice and funny.

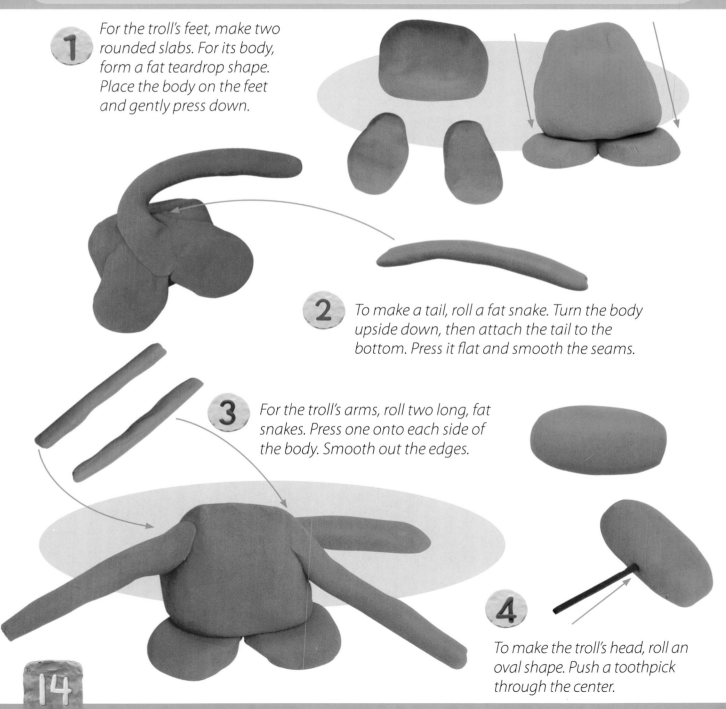

1 *For the troll's feet, make two rounded slabs. For its body, form a fat teardrop shape. Place the body on the feet and gently press down.*

2 *To make a tail, roll a fat snake. Turn the body upside down, then attach the tail to the bottom. Press it flat and smooth the seams.*

3 *For the troll's arms, roll two long, fat snakes. Press one onto each side of the body. Smooth out the edges.*

4 *To make the troll's head, roll an oval shape. Push a toothpick through the center.*

5 For ears, make two pointed ovals. Attach one to each side of the head. Then attach the head to the body.

6 Make two eyes (see page 10 for instructions). Press the eyes onto the troll's face.

7 Roll four thin snakes. Make two blue and two purple. Loop one snake of each color around the troll's wrist and ear. Repeat this step for the other side.

8 Roll four thin, short snakes using blue, purple, yellow, and green clay. Curve each snake and press them together to make a rainbow. Flatten the rainbow and press it onto the troll's belly.

Claymation Tip
When animating your troll, it can slowly waddle across the set. Its tail can swish from side to side. Make several puppets to create a band of brightly colored trolls.

Stick Puppet

One of the first stars of clay animation was Gumby, a flat stick figure. He was created by animator Art Clokey in the 1950s. The popular character went on to star in his own TV show and movies. This monster puppet is created in the same style as Gumby.

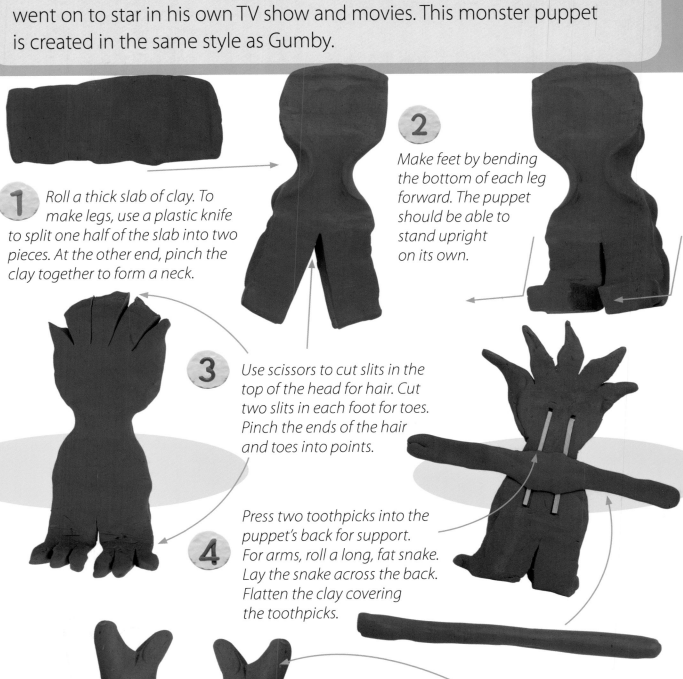

1 *Roll a thick slab of clay. To make legs, use a plastic knife to split one half of the slab into two pieces. At the other end, pinch the clay together to form a neck.*

2 *Make feet by bending the bottom of each leg forward. The puppet should be able to stand upright on its own.*

3 *Use scissors to cut slits in the top of the head for hair. Cut two slits in each foot for toes. Pinch the ends of the hair and toes into points.*

4 *Press two toothpicks into the puppet's back for support. For arms, roll a long, fat snake. Lay the snake across the back. Flatten the clay covering the toothpicks.*

5 *To make hands, pinch out two fingers at the end of each arm.*

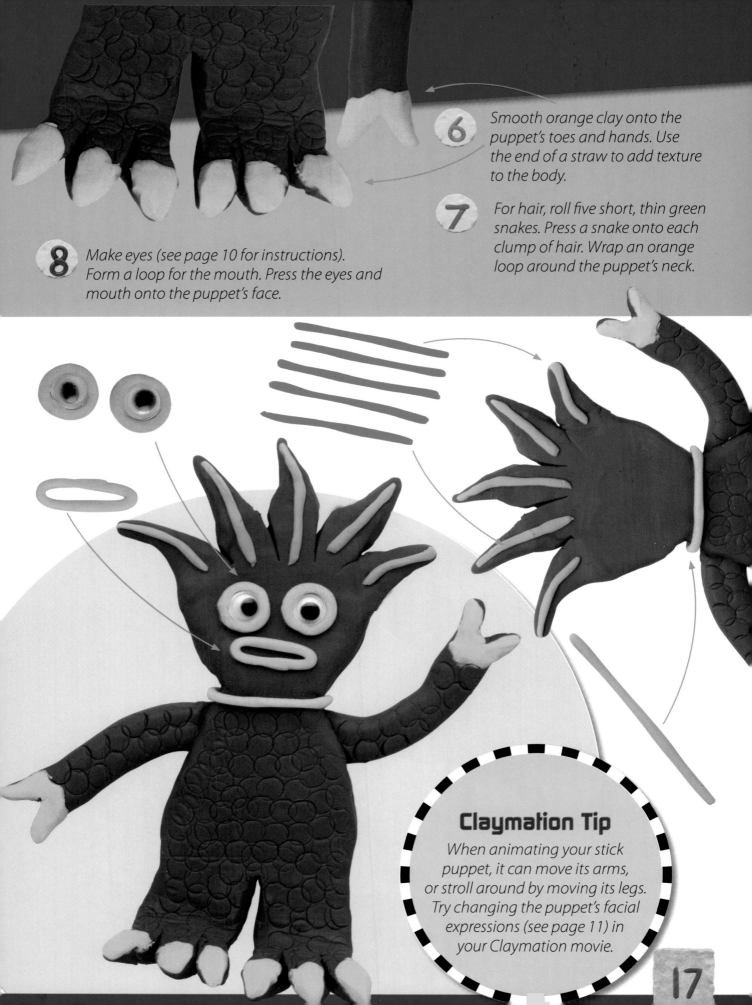

6 Smooth orange clay onto the puppet's toes and hands. Use the end of a straw to add texture to the body.

7 For hair, roll five short, thin green snakes. Press a snake onto each clump of hair. Wrap an orange loop around the puppet's neck.

8 Make eyes (see page 10 for instructions). Form a loop for the mouth. Press the eyes and mouth onto the puppet's face.

Claymation Tip

When animating your stick puppet, it can move its arms, or stroll around by moving its legs. Try changing the puppet's facial expressions (see page 11) in your Claymation movie.

Mummy Puppet

Mummies are corpses that have been carefully preserved. A mummy's body is wrapped in long bands of cloth. The ancient Egyptians mummified people for over 3,000 years. In scary movies, mummies are often brought back to life.

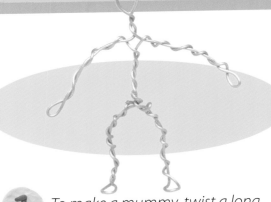

1 To make a mummy, twist a long piece of wire into an armature as shown on page 9.

2 Use a foam ball for the mummy's head. Use a plastic knife to cut a slit in the foam. Press the foam onto the top loop of the armature.

3 Soften a large ball of brown clay. Completely cover the armature, but leave the feet uncovered. Add extra clay to fill out the body. Keep adding clay and smoothing the body until you are happy with the mummy's shape.

4 To make feet, roll two oval shapes. Press one foot onto each of the wire feet. Fold the clay to cover the wire.

5 Make two eyes (see page 10 for instructions). Press the eyes onto the mummy's face.

6 Knead together some orange and white clay. Press out a large, flat, thin pancake shape. Use the plastic knife to cut the pancake into long, thin strips. You could also create strips by rolling and flattening several snakes out of the clay.

7 Wind the strips around the puppet's body. Make sure you can still see the mummy's eyes. (The model shows thin strips but you could use wider strips as well to speed up the wrapping process.)

Claymation Tip

Your mummy puppet can stiffly limp across your set. Position its arms straight out to mimic the traditional way a mummy walks in scary movies.

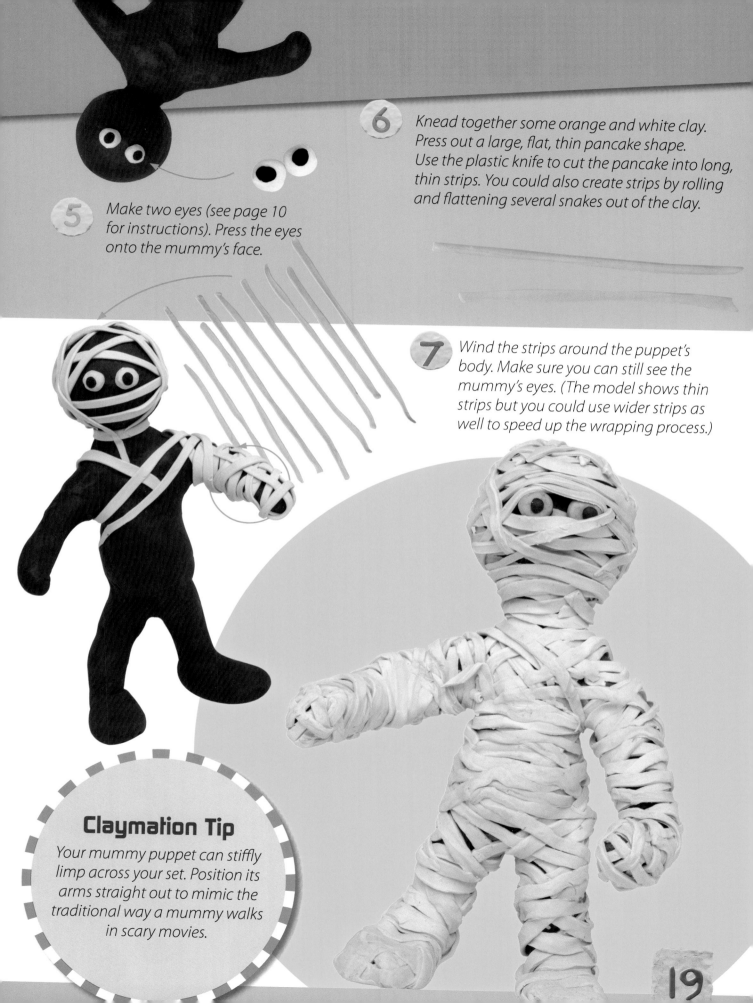

Zombie Puppet

Zombies, also known as the walking dead, are another monster featured in many horror and fantasy movies. They are the corpses of people that have been brought back to life. Zombies moan and walk around in a trancelike state.

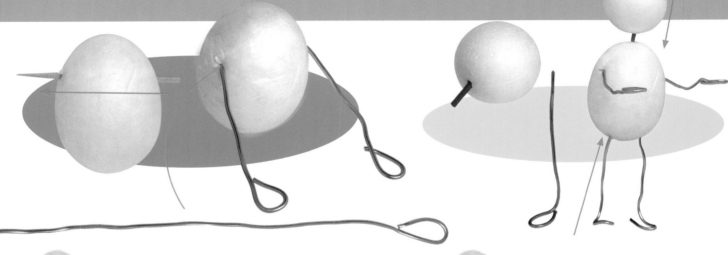

1 Use an egg-shaped foam ball for the zombie's body. Use a toothpick to poke a hole through the top. For the arms, cut a long piece of craft wire. Make a loop at one end, then thread the wire through the hole. Form another loop at the other end. Bend the arms forward.

2 Push a toothpick into a round ball for the head. Cut two pieces of wire for legs. Make loops for feet. Attach the head and legs to the body.

3 Use beige clay to cover the armature. Leave the feet uncovered. For shoes, form two oval slabs. Press the wire feet into the shoes. Fold the clay over the wire and smooth the seams.

4 Press out a large, thin slab of blue clay. Wrap it around the zombie's waist. Use scissors to cut a slit down the center of the front and back. To make pants, pinch the edges together around each leg. Leave the bottom ragged.

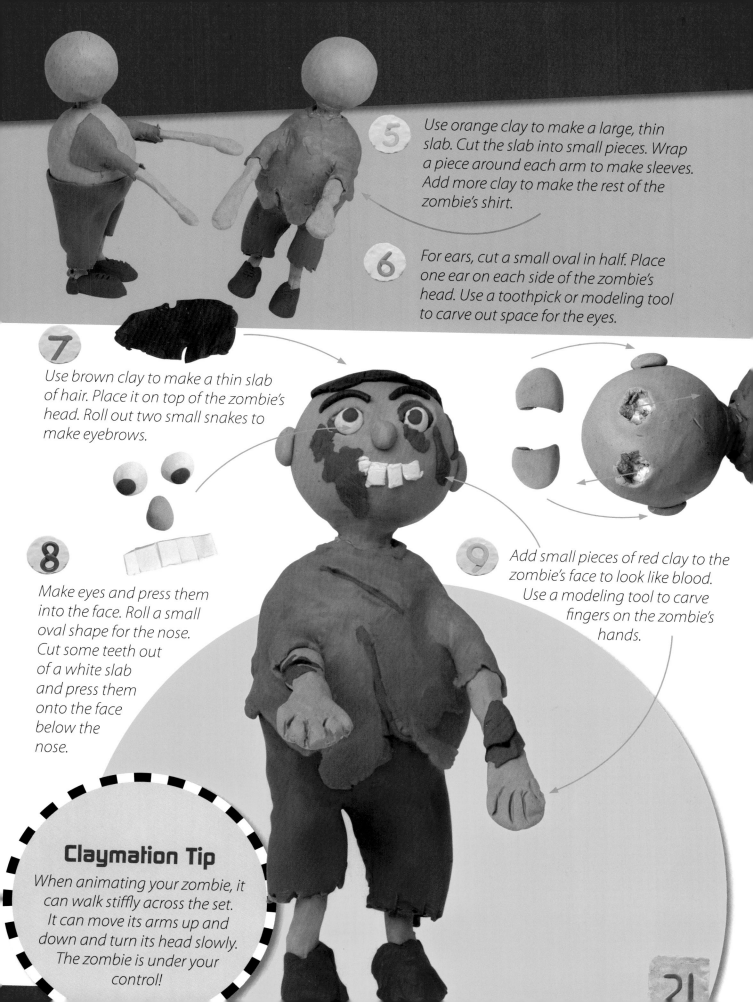

5 Use orange clay to make a large, thin slab. Cut the slab into small pieces. Wrap a piece around each arm to make sleeves. Add more clay to make the rest of the zombie's shirt.

6 For ears, cut a small oval in half. Place one ear on each side of the zombie's head. Use a toothpick or modeling tool to carve out space for the eyes.

7 Use brown clay to make a thin slab of hair. Place it on top of the zombie's head. Roll out two small snakes to make eyebrows.

8 Make eyes and press them into the face. Roll a small oval shape for the nose. Cut some teeth out of a white slab and press them onto the face below the nose.

9 Add small pieces of red clay to the zombie's face to look like blood. Use a modeling tool to carve fingers on the zombie's hands.

Claymation Tip
When animating your zombie, it can walk stiffly across the set. It can move its arms up and down and turn its head slowly. The zombie is under your control!

Ogre Puppet

For centuries, ogres have appeared in fairy tales and folklore from around the world. In stories, ogres often eat humans. These giant monsters have green-colored skin and unusually large heads. Cyclops is a man-eating ogre from Greek mythology that had one eye in the middle of his forehead. Other ogres, like Shrek, are friendly.

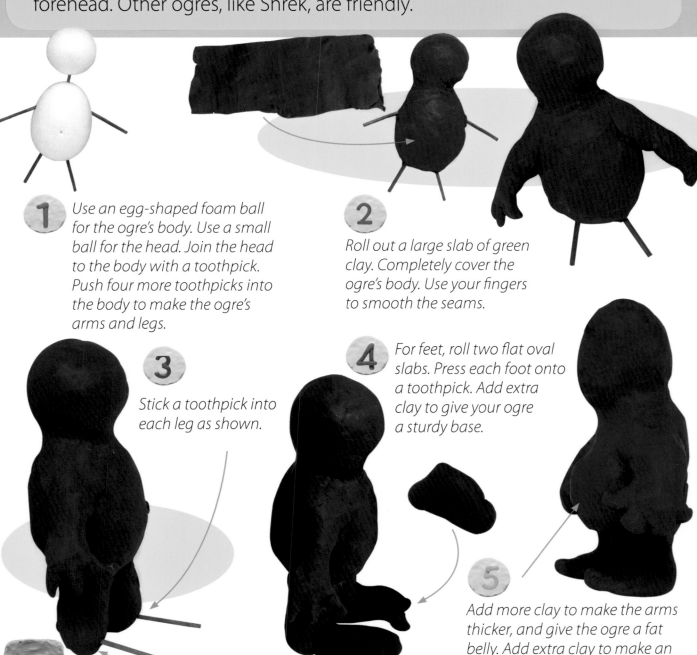

1 Use an egg-shaped foam ball for the ogre's body. Use a small ball for the head. Join the head to the body with a toothpick. Push four more toothpicks into the body to make the ogre's arms and legs.

2 Roll out a large slab of green clay. Completely cover the ogre's body. Use your fingers to smooth the seams.

3 Stick a toothpick into each leg as shown.

4 For feet, roll two flat oval slabs. Press each foot onto a toothpick. Add extra clay to give your ogre a sturdy base.

5 Add more clay to make the arms thicker, and give the ogre a fat belly. Add extra clay to make an oversized head.

6 Use a modeling tool to carve out a mouth and to make an eye socket. Use green clay to make two pointed ears. Press one ear onto each side of the head.

7 Make an eye (see page 10) and place it in the eye socket. Roll a horn and press it onto the top of the ogre's head. Mold a single brown tooth and press it into the roof of the ogre's mouth.

8 To make a necklace, wrap a loop around the ogre's neck. Press a flattened ball and teeth onto the loop.

9 For an armband, roll and flatten a beige snake. Decorate the band with flattened yellow balls. Wrap it around the ogre's wrist.

10 To create a loincloth, roll and flatten a brown snake. Use the plastic knife to cut out small triangles along one edge. Press the loincloth around the ogre's waist.

Claymation Tip

In your movie, make the ogre slowly sneak up on other characters. Use a thin green pancake to make an eyelid. Remove the clay between frames to make the monster's eye blink.

The Props

Props are used in the creation of the movie. They decorate the set. Props add visual interest to the movie. Sometimes the puppets interact with them. Brainstorm ideas about what you might see in a spooky monster movie.

1 *Make a ghost out of a flat, round piece of clay. Build a base for the ghost by sticking a toothpick into a clump of clay. Attach a foam ball to the other end of the toothpick. Drape the round piece of clay over the ball. Add two eyes.*

2 *Use a small slab of clay to make a tombstone. Round the corners. Flatten the bottom so it will stand on its own. Make letters from snake shapes. You can also make a tombstone out of cardboard. Use a black marker to write words on the stone. Make grass to support the stone by using scissors to fringe green clay.*

RIP

SWEET
PEEK·A·B
1737 - 1877

SCARRY
KAT
1890-91

3 *Use a twig to make a tree. Stick one end into a ball of clay. Add grass to hide the base. You can have a single tree on your set or use several to build a haunted forest.*

4 Make a spooky bat to hang on your set. Press out a long, thin brown slab. Add a brown ball in the middle. Pinch out a wing on each side of the ball. Use a long, thin gray snake to hang the bat from a branch on your set.

5 Use stretched-out cotton balls to make misty clouds. Use loops of white tape to attach the clouds to the set.

6 Make a full moon from a white pancake shape. Pinch the clay to add texture. Use any leftover clay to build a statue to set in front of a tombstone.

7 Create a creepy spider's web. Roll out several thin white snakes. To make the web, form a triangle then lay out the snakes in a crisscross pattern as shown. Add extra clay to the corners to attach the web to the set.

Claymation Tip

Use two magnets to animate your moon. Press one magnet into the back of the moon. When you're ready to start shooting frames, place the moon on the front of the set. Match the other magnet on the other side. You can now make the moon drift slowly across the sky in your film.

8 Combine any leftover clay. Roll out several thin pieces to make stones. Place the stones together to build a pathway.

The Set

The set is where you will film your movie. It is the landscape in which your story will come to life. A set can be as simple as a piece of paper taped to the wall or more complex. The set needs to be large enough for your puppets to be able to move around.

Basic Set

The most basic set is a single piece of paper or poster board. Tape one end of the paper to the wall. Pull the paper and tape the other end to the table. Leave a bit of a curve in the paper.

1 *You can build a simple set using pieces of cardboard. Start with two large rectangles that are the same size. Line up the long sides of the rectangles and tape them together.*

2 *Cut a triangle out of cardboard.*

3 *Tape the triangle to the back of one rectangle. Bend the other to form an L shape as shown.*

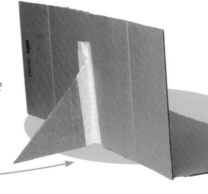

4 *Fold a piece of colored paper over the top of the box. Use clear or double-sided tape to secure each end of the paper to the front and back of the set.*

5   You can also make a set from black foam board. Take a large piece of board and bend it in half. Tape together two pieces of foam board for a larger set.

Try This!

Make a haunted house from pieces of cardboard. Decorate the house with markers and paint. Use tape to attach the house to the set.

6   Use cardboard to make a triangle. Tape the triangle to the back of one rectangle. Bend the other rectangle to form an L shape as shown.

Alternative Set

You can paint a background directly on the cardboard or paint a white piece of poster board and attach it to the cardboard.

7   Arrange your props. Before you start shooting, secure the set to the surface you are working on with tape.

27

Lights, Camera, . . .

To light your set, a couple of desk lamps or the overhead lights should do the trick. Don't place your set near a window or shoot outside unless it is an overcast day. Changes in lighting will cause flickering in your movie.

Experiment with the placement of the lamps. Take test shots to see how it looks.

Flat, even light is created when two lamps are placed an equal distance apart. There are little or no shadows.

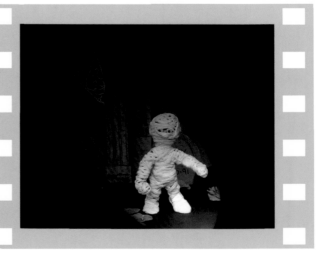

Place your mummy at center stage. Create a spotlight by directing one light onto the set.

28

Claymation does not require a video camera. A digital camera, smartphone camera, or tablet camera will work. Think about the camera angles you want to use while shooting your film. The angle and distance from which you capture your scene can bring your movie to life.

In a straight-on shot, the camera is lined up directly with the puppet.

Shooting the movie from above makes the puppet appear small.

A closeup shot taken from a low angle can create a dramatic effect.

. . . Action!
Making Your Movie

It's time to make your Claymation movie! You have your storyboard, your puppet(s), your set, lights, and camera. Position the puppets on the set when you are ready to begin. Using your storyboard as a guide, start taking photos. Make sure you move your puppets in very tiny increments. The smaller the movements, the smoother the film will be. Be careful not to move the camera while taking a sequence of shots.

You can use a camera on a tripod and import your stills later into an animation program. Or you can use your smartphone or tablet camera to capture photos directly in a stop-motion animation app.

Make sure your hands are out of the frame after moving the puppet before taking the next shot.

It takes a lot of patience to make a Claymation film. Slowly move your puppet toward an object on your set to make it appear as if the puppet is moving on its own. If the puppet moves too far in each shot it will appear to jump rather than move in one fluid motion.

Now it's time to finish your movie. **Postproduction** is the last step in creating your Claymation film. Within your app or animation program you can edit your frames, removing any that don't work. This is also the time to add music or sound effects. Music can set the mood of the film. Different types of music can sound happy, sad, or suspenseful. There are all kinds of free sound effects on the Internet, or you can record your own. Adding effects to your movie will bring the action to life.

Finally, it's showtime! Stage a spooky screening to share your monster Claymation with an audience. At the end, take a bow!

If there is a scene that doesn't work, cut it!

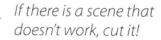

Use clay letters to make credits for your movie. Include a title and end credits, listing yourself and anyone else who helped.

GLOSSARY

animation In film, creating the illusion of movement using still images played in a rapid sequence.

armature A wire frame that acts as a skeleton for a sculpture made with modeling clay.

frame An individual picture in a series of images.

postproduction The final stages of finishing a movie after it has been recorded that usually involves editing and adding sound.

stop-motion An animation technique that uses a series of shots showing small movements to make characters or objects appear to move.

storyboard A series of pictures that show the scenes in an animation.

FOR MORE INFORMATION

FURTHER READING

Cassidy, John, and Nicholas Berger. *The Klutz Book of Animation.*
Palo Alto, CA: Klutz, 2010.

Grabham, Tim. *Movie Maker: The Ultimate Guide to Making Films*
Somerville, MA: Candlewick, 2010.

Piercy, Helen. *Animation Studio.*
Somerville, MA: Candlewick, 2013.

WEBSITES

For web resources related to the subject of this book, go to:
www.windmillbooks.com/weblinks and select this book's title.

INDEX

A
armature(s) 6, 8, 9, 18, 20
C
camera 4, 29, 30
F
frames 4, 5, 11, 23, 25, 31
L
lights 28, 30

M
modeling clay 4, 6, 8
P
postproduction 31
props 24
S
set 6, 15, 19, 21, 24, 25, 26, 27, 28, 30, 31

smartphone 4, 29, 30
stop-motion animation 4, 30
storyboard 5, 30
T
tablet 4, 29, 30